KHAKUN SHRUGS

AF772425

A Thennla Scenario for MYTHRAS

By
Bruce Turner

Cartography by Simon Bray
Cover by Jethro Lentle

Playtesters

Patrick Davis, Paul Dawson, Douglas Dea,Ben Engquist, Chris Kanute,

Ernest Mueller, Jim Pope, Paul Richmond, Tim Rudloff

Published under license in the UK by Aeon Games Publishing
www.aeongamespublishing.co.uk

ISBN 978-1-91147-121-9

Printed in Great Britain

THE DESIGN MECHANISM

Mythras

Khakun Shrugs

The Taskan Empire has embarked upon a massive campaign to reconstruct Further Tarsenia following the devastation wrought by the Sheng savages twenty years ago. Part of this is the reopening of the silver mines at Seppesh. The Sheng left the old city a blackened ruin and earthquakes buried the old mines shortly afterwards. Now the mines are running again and the city of New Seppesh is a ramshackle frontier settlement of colonists and misfits from across the Taskan Empire, eager to get rich from the mines. Last month, miners heard rumbling underneath Mount Khakun; then, last week, the mountain gave a massive shrug. Today, the miners refuse to go underground. The Tarsen priest, Michel Tob, is organising an expedition into the long-abandoned Mountain Foot shrine to see if it can be reopened and the mountain appeased.

Khakun Shrugs is a Mythras adventure set in the world of Thennla, detailed in the Shores of Korantia and the Taskan Empire supplements. The scenario assumes that the characters are colonists and residents of New Seppesh, or visitors to it for one reason or another. They are linked to a local priest of Tarsen through his Ruddy River Association (a combination of magical cabal and drinking club), but may originally hail from all manner of lands both inside and outside the Taskan Empire (such as Korantia).

While intended for Thennla, the scenario can fit into world where magic is reasonably common and myths are powerful. It will make a good addition to The Realm, as found in Book of Quests, with the mountain located in the range bordering the Long Riding, south west of Cylder.

Adventure Structure

This is a straightforward adventure, moving from one scene to another in linear fashion:

- The Ruddy River Association Meets
- The expedition travels to the base of Mount Khakun. Along the way they find some interesting ruins, and a woodcutter who can tell them that there are Sheng nomads in the area.
- The characters encounter the Drumming Camp the Sheng nomads have been using to inflame the giant Khakun's dreams. They drive off the nomads and stop the drumming.
- The characters finally reach the base of Mount Khakun. A strenuous climb is needed to reach the Mountain Foot Temple. A short-faced bear mother and her two cubs occupy the temple and must be cleared out before safe access is possible – it is evident that the nomads have attempted access, as the bears killed one of them and wounded some others.
- The characters enter the inner sanctum of the Mountain Foot Temple. With Michel Tob's help, they start the ritual and evoke the Nightmares of the giant Khakun. The Nightmares completely possess a convict Michel Tob brought along to serve in the role of opponent. Additionally, nomads who have embodied the Nightmares attack the rest of the group (primarily the Taskan militia brought along as escorts) outside the temple. By the end,

the giant Khakun has been sent back to sleep, the Nightmares have been driven off, and the characters have been able to reestablish the propitiation ritual that keeps the mountain stable.

There are a number of ways the adventure could deviate from this path. Most obviously the characters could either bypass, or be defeated by, any number of the opponents they encounter. They could also fail to locate the shrine. The simplest approach to dealing with this kind of mischance is to allow the characters to become somewhat lost on the slopes of Mount Khakun, whereupon either they find the shrine, or a rift in the side of the mountain spewing foul vapors that can serve in the same role as the shrine.

History & Mythology

The old Tarsen city of Seppesh was established along the Ruddy River in large part due to the discovery of silver deposits in the roots of Mount Khakun. Mining the silver was complicated by the fact that the mountain was notably unstable, prone to frequent earth tremors that collapsed mine works and buried settlements. Tarsen discovered that the mountain was actually the sleeping giant Khakun the Silver-Belted, and that the silver mine was drawing ore out of the links of his belt. He was able to negotiate with the giant, and drew upon the old story of How the Giant's Daughter Calmed His Sleep to work out an arrangement that would keep the giant slumbering, stabilise the mountain, and allow the miners to work. The cult of Tarsen established the Mountain Foot Temple to carry out the necessary rites every year.

When the Sheng nomads rampaged through Further Tarsenia twenty years ago, Seppesh was not spared. The nomads put the city to the torch, killing or carrying off most of the population. The annual rituals failed and, not long after the nomads departed the area, Mount Khakun shuddered in a protest that buried the old mines, half of the city, and the Mountain Foot Temple. The few survivors fled down the Ruddy River, looking for refuge in the coastal settlements.

Ten years ago the Taskan Empire sent the first colonists up the river to reconstruct the city and reopen the mines. New Seppesh has since become a significant settlement, though it still lacks any of the grace and sophistication of the original city. It is a ramshackle place of hastily-constructed buildings behind a wooden palisade. Only the twin temples of Tarsen and Zygas Taga show any permanence – they were constructed from stone blocks dragged from the original city site, including some pieces of the original buried temples. The colonists were supported by the Empire and concerned themselves primarily with re-establishing agriculture on large land grants along the river, and with rebuilding the city.

Three years ago miners returned to New Seppesh to reopen the silver mines. Last year, they found the ruins of the original mine shaft and were able to bring up a small quantity of silver ore. It was only a month ago that the rumblings in the mountain started; nobody has been harmed yet, but there are survivors from the original city among the miners and they have persuaded their fellows that the old rituals must be reestablished or disaster will follow.

Khakun the Silver Belted

The great giant Khakun the Silver-Belted was hungry. He looked about and saw a herd of sheep grazing in the pastures below his seat. He gathered them up, roasted them whole upon a fire built from a thousand trees, and gobbled them all down. His hunger sated, he settled upon his stony couch but could not find sleep. His daughter, Okonia the Raven Tressed, knew that his unrest was caused by the struggles of the sheep in his belly and sought to ease his torment. First she brought him fine delicacies to settle his stomach. The kicking and thrashing of the sheep diminished, yet he still could not sleep. So Okonia sang to him, a pleasant song that drove wakefulness away. Yet silver-belted Khakun's sleep was still not restful, he turned and tossed. Okonia looked in his ear and saw that he was troubled by awful nightmares. She brought out a brazier and placed coals from the fire into it. Upon them she laved scented oils and placed exotic incense. The heavy smokes and steams drifted into silver-belted Khakun's nose and ears and pulled out the Nightmares. The Nightmares fought, but raven-tressed Okonia was ready for them. She cast her silken shawl over them, holding them in place with its tight weave. She drew out her bright-edged dagger and stabbed them, and then flung them into the coals to burn away. And when the last of the coals turned to ash, her father breathed easily and settled into pleasant sleep.

The Ruddy River Association

Michel Tob is a ranking priest of Tarsen in New Seppesh, and the leader of the Ruddy River Association. He established the Association shortly after his arrival in New Seppesh as a way to bring some of the more unusual members of the new community into the congregation of Tarsen, and as a way to ensure that appropriate worship was given to the lesser-known members of the Tarsenian pantheon. The Association meets in the courtyard of Tob's home next to the new Temple of Tarsen, and the priest makes a point of ensuring that there is always beer available for the meetings.

Today the Association has a membership of eight people. Few of them are prominent members of the community in the normal sense, but all of them pass the priest's judgment as being worthy of notice. His informal requirements for membership are:

- At least one skill of any kind at 70% or higher
- At least 40% skill in spoken Tarsenian
- At least 20% Literacy

Two members of the Association (Michel Tob and the Thesh priest Ulvikus Ekaloon) are able to teach Taskan Rites and some folk magic spells:

Bladesharp, Bludgeon, Calculate, Disruption, Heal, Ignite, Lock, Repair

The Association demands a payment of 50 taskeens for each spell taught (half of which goes to the teacher). It also requires dues of 10 taskeens every season (most of which Michel spends on beer).

The Expedition

If the characters are outsiders, or newly arrived in New Seppesh, it doesn't take long for word to reach them that Michel Tob is looking for help in stablising Mount Khakun. Tob hoists the association flag on top of his house and sounds the bell in the plaza in front of the Temple of Tarsen – the usual signal for the Association to meet. When everyone is assembled, he explains the situation: Mount Khakun is obviously unstable and the miners are refusing to go into the mines. Even the people of New Seppesh are concerned, because the last time the mountain had a severe quake, the landslides buried half of the old city.

Tob tells the members of the Association that he has been reviewing old records recovered both from the ruins of the temple in Seppesh (which took some digging) and sent to him from the Imperial Library of Ralmyra (which drew most of its holdings from scrolls unearthed from that city's ruins). He has found both the story of the Giant's Daughter and information on how the original priests of Tarsen at Seppesh propitiated the giant Khakun. He tells the members that he is organising an expedition to the site of the old Mountain Foot Temple. The goal is to reopen the buried temple and perform a ritual to calm the giant, reestablishing the propitiation rites that kept the original city and mines safe. He asks that the members of the association, or any willing adventurers, accompany him on the expedition.

Michel Tob's expectation is that all of the members will be willing to join the expedition. The only exception is old Ulvikus Ekaloon: even though he is a survivor of Seppesh, he is now of quite advanced age and lost a leg in the original disaster. Michel Tob does not offer financial payment to anyone for the trip, though he is willing (if asked) to provide provisions for the day or so it will take to reach the original temple site. If any characters are reluctant to join him, he tries to appeal to their (possibly nonexistent) sense of duty to New Seppesh, to their loyalty to Emperor Zygas Taga, to their sense of adventure, to the fact that not going is base cowardice, and finally to the fact that they (may) have property in or around the city whose value could be harmed by an earthquake. If none of that is enough to convince a character of the worth of the expedition, or if he can be persuaded with a Hard Influence roll opposed by Tob's Willpower, he grudgingly agrees to pay 2 Taskeens per day if a character succeeds, and 3 Taskeens per day if the success is critical.

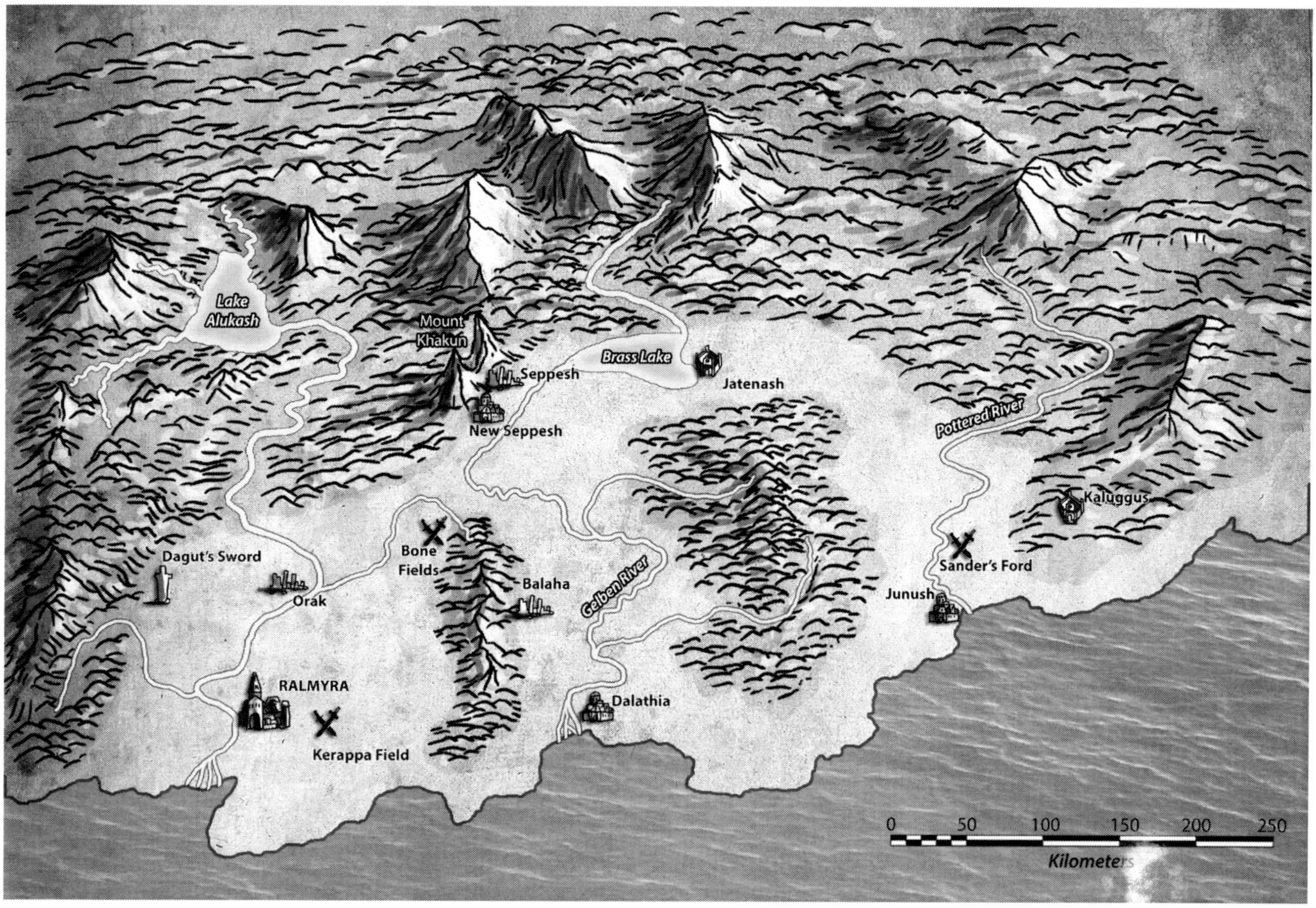

Composition

The entire group that is heading to the Mountain Foot Temple is quite large. It includes:

- ***Michel Tob***, the priest of Tarsen and nominal leader of the expedition.
- ***The characters***
- ***Captain Varhalle Eghis***, an officer from the Taskan army and leader of the militia
- ***Habalbus Narassia***, a Taskan military sorcerer attached to the militia
- ***A dozen Taskan militia*** from New Seppesh, armed with spears and shields
- ***Terceris Yando***, a convicted thief from New Seppesh. He has a role to play in the ritual to calm the giant.

Varhalle Eghis is a stern-faced officer with experience leading Taskan regulars against Thennalt barbarians. He seems somewhat bitter about being stationed in the northern reaches of the Empire, leading ill-equipped militia.

Terceris Yando may be known to some of the characters as an inveterate hard luck case, a man who doesn't have a straight bone in his body. He has been caught stealing many times, and is usually sentenced to working the mines as punishment. This time, he was apprehended for attacking a local landowner and stealing his elegant walking stick, and he's clearly not going to have the opportunity to work off his crime breaking rocks.

The militiamen are mostly labourers from New Seppesh or small landholders from the outlying settlements. They are equipped with the required minimum kit (spear, shield, dagger). Most of them have at least a leather breastplate (2 points of armor on chest and abdomen). Few have any more than that. They are drilled, but lack discipline.

The Road to the Mountain Foot Temple

The Mountain Foot Temple is about a day's travel from New Seppesh. At one time there was a moderately-marked road between the temple and the old city, but it hasn't been used for

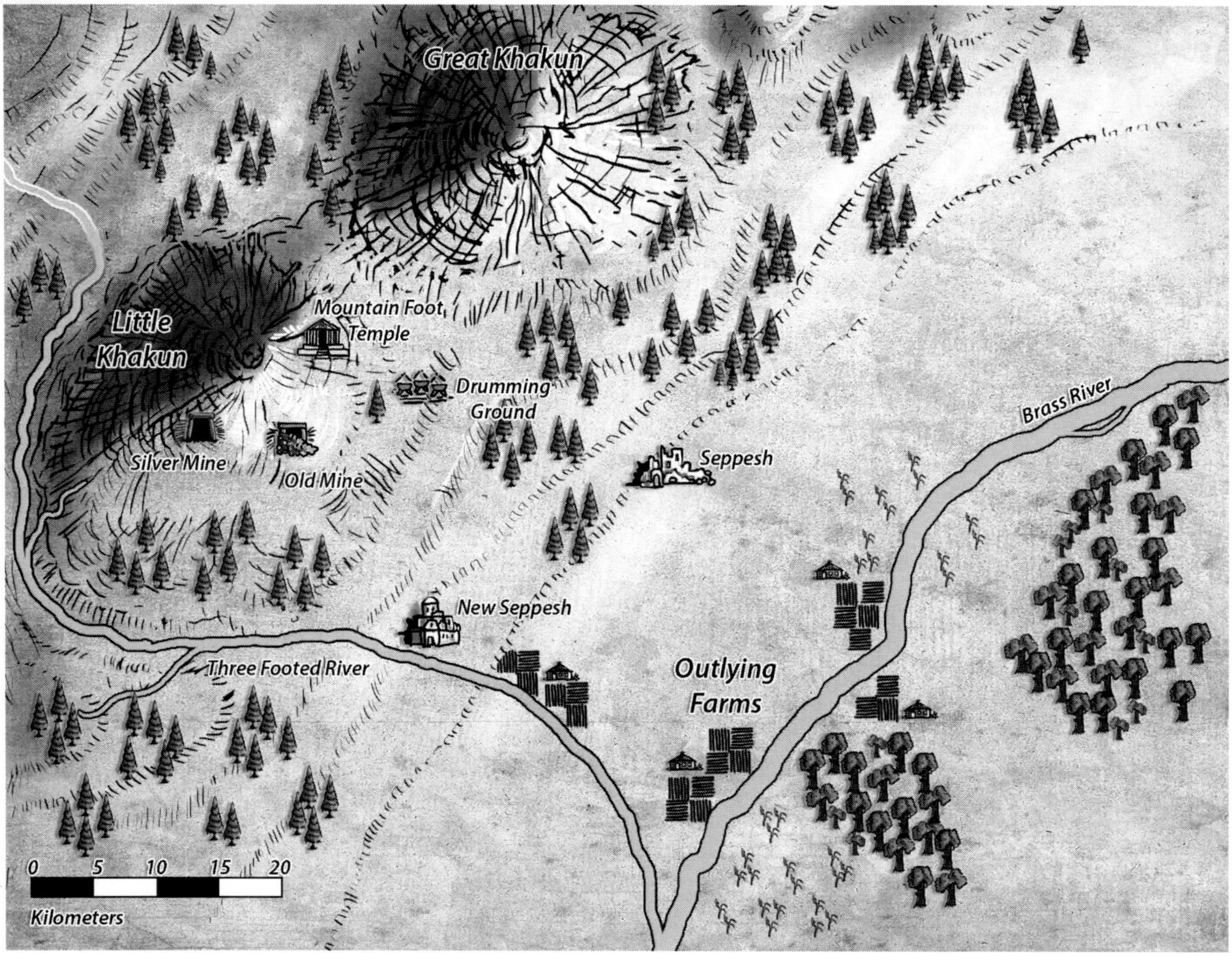

twenty years and, except for the sections buried by landslides, is heavily overgrown. The overall experience is an overland trek, except that the characters occasionally encounter ruined buildings (small hamlets, way stations, inns) as long as they are close to the original path.

There are three important roles for the journey: Scout, Navigator, and Trailbreaker. The key skills for each are:

- ***Navigator***: Navigate or Locale (Hard) - Determine location and destination
- ***Scout***: Locale or Perception - Identify promising routes
- ***Trailbreaker***: Brawn or Endurance (Hard) - Clear obstacles from the route

Reaching the base of Mount Khakun and the path up to the Mountain Foot Temple is an extended task requiring a score of 100% or higher to succeed. Each attempt requires six hours of effort. Progress is based upon the results of the three characters' skill rolls:

1. The Navigator starts the sequence. Success gives +25% progress towards the goal and reduces the Scout's difficulty grade by one. Critical success gives +50% and reduces the Scout's difficulty grade by two. A fumble increases the difficulty grade by one.
2. The Scout follows the Navigator. Success gives +25% progress towards the goal. Critical success gives +50% progress towards the goal. Failure gives +0%, and a fumble reduces progress by -25%.
3. The Trailbreaker follows the Scout, and may only roll if the Scout succeeded. Success increases the progress gained by +25%. Critical success increases the progress gained by +50%. A fumble forces the Trailbreaker to make an Endurance or Evade roll or suffer 1d6 damage to a random hit location (no armor).

After two attempts, all members of the party must make an Endurance roll or lose a fatigue level. Resting for three hours regains the loss. Once the party reaches 100% progress, it has reached the foot of Mount Khakun.

The Woodcutter

Not long after setting out the characters meet a local woodcutter. He is adjusting a substantial load of cut boughs and explains that he and his cousins are assembling a charcoal burn nearby. If the characters offer to help him with the load, he warns them that he has seen Sheng raiders around. Even worse, late at night, while watching the charcoal burn, his cousins have seen fearsome black spirit-shapes drifting through the woods. As he describes the shapes, he makes a gesture of blessing and touches a necklace carved in the likeness of Tarsen.

Tob and Varhalle Eghis are reluctant to pause and help this woodcutter, but the information he has is genuine and useful. Tob petulantly tells the characters they can pause if they want to, but will need to catch up with the rest of the expedition because he does not intend to divert. He may even threaten to deduct any delay from the characters' pay, if they have negotiated a financial settlement from him. The woodcutter is grateful for any offer of help and assures the characters that he can manage his load; his gratitude is the information about the Sheng and the spirit forms.

The Ruined Inn

Midway through their progress the expedition reaches a ruined inn, only its exterior walls, made of strong stone, remaining. Searching the ruins uncovers the below items, with one successful Perception roll required for each item:

- Three pots of old wine, somewhat vinegary but still quite drinkable.
- A small gold statuette of an eagle, worth 50 taskeens.
- A broken spear haft of Sheng construction, quite recent in construction.

Even in its broken state, the inn is sheltered from the elements and is a good place to rest. Friendly spirits lived here once (the remains of a shrine are visible in a corner) and still visit from time to time. Staying here for at least an hour restores a fatigue level and a Magic Point.

The Drumming Grounds

As the characters draw near to the foot of the mountain, the sound of drumming is detectable. The drumming gradually becomes too loud to ignore, and the source becomes obvious: a clearing on the slope, surrounded by three bonfires, with a group of Sheng nomads milling about, mostly on foot. Their horses are tied up around the edges of the clearing, and the nomads form three groups:

- Sentries on foot, ranging around the edges of the clearing. There are as many sentries as there are characters.
- Eight drummers, hammering away at four huge drums made from horsehide.
- The leader, Draubalhut, overseeing the ceremony
- Several onlookers, exhausted former drummers waiting their turns and otherwise uninvolved nomads who are cheering their comrades on. There are four exhausted drummers, plus as many onlookers as there are Taskan militia with the characters.

The Sheng nomads' task is to unsettle the giant Khakun with their drumming ritual, which recalls the myth *The Giant Visits*

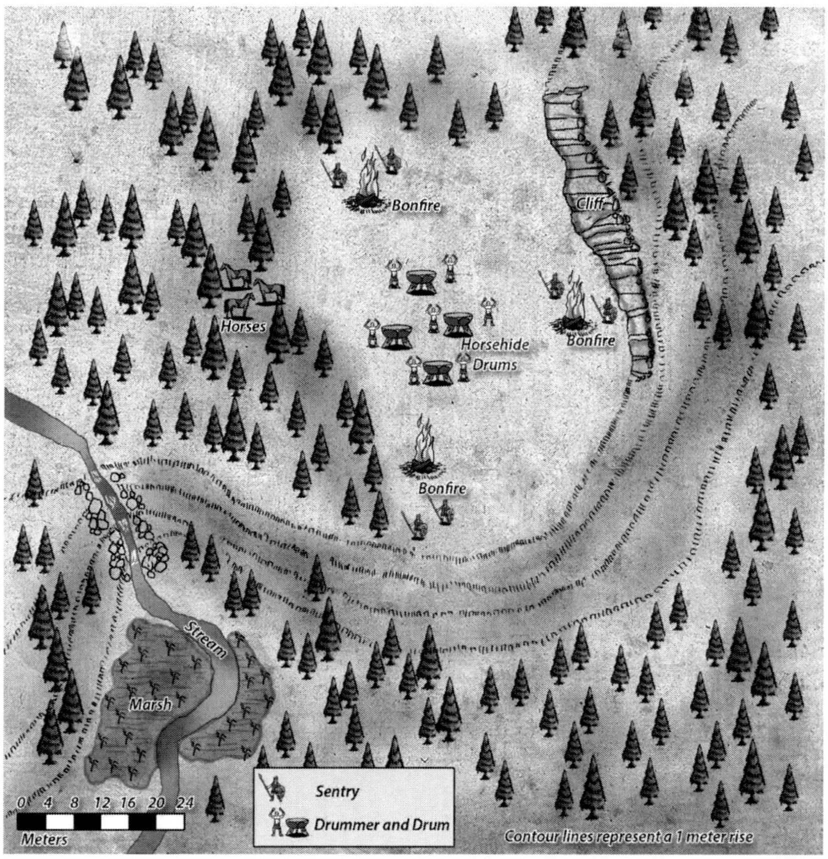

the Valley, describing how thunder annoyed silver-belted Khakun, enough that he stomped his way down among the valley people who were talking to the Thunder Ram.

If the characters and the expedition decide to intervene, the Sheng nomads are not interested in a violent confrontation. They have a few Alarm spells set on the approaches to their camp, and the characters' group is large enough that someone will trip at least one of them. With forewarning, the nomads mount up and ride off, leaving their drums and bonfires behind. If the expedition opts to engage the Sheng in daylight, Draubalhut and 1d6+2 additional nomads remain close enough to take parting shots at the expedition, firing from long range. Even in darkness, Draubalhut fires twice at the characters after casting his Twilight Sight spell (limiting darkness penalties to one grade – the characters will be able to see his eyes burn with pale fire). After one volley, the nomads ride off around the mountain. Characters with bows are welcome to return fire. If the characters force an engagement, Draubalhut and his immediate retinue are prepared to fight.

The nomads have not spent long at the Drumming Ground. The four drums consist of horsehide stretched over an open wooden frame, easy to put together and carry on horseback. The other items left behind are mostly small personal effects and bits of food.

Mountain Foot Temple

At one time the Mountain Foot Temple was a magnificent structure; a great stone building surrounded by columns, and raised-up on a stone platform with a broad stairway to the main door. Inside, a huge statue of Khakun was flanked by a slightly smaller statue of Tarsen. The priests of Tarsen in charge of propitiating the mountain would address those selected to participate in the ritual from the altar beneath the giant's feet, and then descend into the inner shrine for the secret portions of the ceremony.

The temple was partially spared destruction at the hands of the earthquakes and landslides that devastated the old city of Seppesh. Much of the structure is buried beneath stone and rubble, and part of it is collapsed. The statue of Khakun is buried and the statue of Tarsen is completely shattered. Until recently the access to the inner shrine was blocked off by rubble, but the recent tremors have cleared the way again.

The militia and their Captain are unwilling to enter the temple. Varhalle Eghis insists that the priest and the characters are the ones who signed up to negotiate with a mountain. The militia is there to keep nomads away and act as a lay chorus (to donate Magic Points if the priest needs them), not to venture into abandoned temples. This may cause some friction with the characters, and Tob is disgruntled at Varhalle Eghis's reluctance, but for the sake of expediency agrees the can remain outside, guarding against the return of the Sheng nomads.

Searching the area outside the entrance can be carried out with either Perception or Track rolls. Either uncovers signs of a struggle, and, not far from the entrance, what are clearly human remains (part of an arm, seemingly torn-off at the elbow, teeth, and scraps of bloody clothing). A Track or Lore (Animals) roll reveals the tracks as those of a large bear, and the remains are part of a recent meal. The tracks clearly lead into the temple.

There are double doors at the back of the temple leading to a carved, sloping passage. The passage leads to the inner shrine where Michel Tob must perform his ritual.

The Bear Family

The major risks in the outer temple are the short-faced bear and her two cubs, who have taken up residence. They spend much of their time relaxing in the dark corners of the half-collapsed structure, especially now that they have something to eat. Two Sheng nomads (part of the group responsible for the Drumming Ground) attempted to explore the temple some time ago. The bears killed one of them and wounded the other, who managed to reach the inner shrine where the two shades killed him. The bears have dragged the body of the nomad they killed into their nest and have eaten most of it.

The bears regard anyone entering the temple as a potential threat, and definitely a meal. If the characters simply blunder in with limited preparation, the mother bear attacks from surprise with her two cubs on her flanks. The ground within the temple is broken and rough, imposing a level of difficulty on any fighter who does not have the Excellent Footwork combat style trait. The bears are sure-footed and pay no heed to the unstable conditions. The back of the temple is tight and closed, applying another difficulty level to any fighter attempting to use a Long or larger weapon. The two cubs retreat from combat if they are wounded and have a path of escape; however, wounding a cub enrages the mother who, in her ferocious state, gains the modifiers listed below. The mother bear retreats if she believes she has driven-off the invaders, and her cubs are safe. If she is cornered

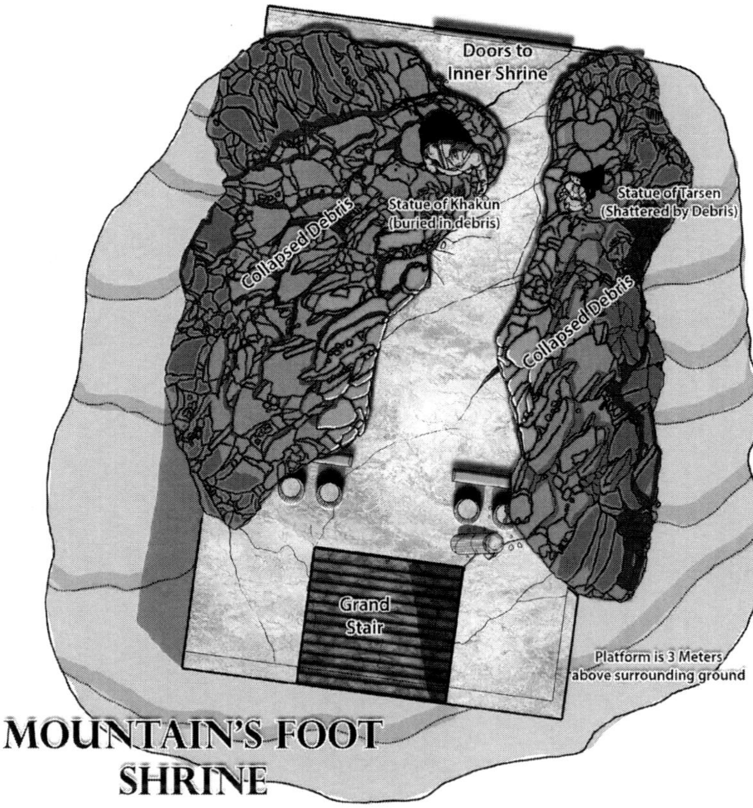

or one of her cubs is hurt or trapped she goes berserk, gaining the following modifiers:

- Increase in Damage Modifier by one step
- Increase in Action Points by one
- Weapon size increased by one step
- Immune to the detrimental effects of Serious Wounds and Fatigue.

Valuables & Rewards

In spite of being a crushed wreck there are some items of worth remaining in the Mountain Foot Temple.

- There are a lot of gold and silver fragments scattered through the temple, the remains of the statues and sacred objects once held here. An hour of searching and a Perception roll uncovers 3d6x10 taskeens worth of pieces. A critical Perception roll finds double the value. After three successful Perception checks there are no more easily-accessible fragments.
- Bear hides are quite valuable and prestigious. If it is recovered in good condition (for example, through a Craft (Butchery) roll) the mother bear's hide is worth at least 200 taskeens. The bear cubs' hides are less valuable, only 50 taskeens each.
- Some of the bas-reliefs along the walls of the temple survived the earthquake. There are four of them. Each is heavy enough that a strong man is needed to carry it (call the militia!) but is worth 400 taskeens or the profound gratitude of the Temple of Tarsen in New Seppesh. A Taskan Rites, Lore (History) or Lore (Art) roll is necessary to identify them.

The Inner Shrine

The inner shrine of the Mountain Foot Temple is a (mostly) natural cave reached through the back of the external temple. Until recently, debris from the old earthquakes closed off access to it, but the recent tremors have unsettled the debris enough that there is space for a man to slip through.

The inner shrine itself is remarkably undamaged. It is dark, but otherwise much as it was when the temple was active. Several massive brass braziers stand at the edges of the cavern. To one side, a small spring flows into a basin that, in turn, empties into a jagged rift running through the back corner of the cavern. An altar stands at the edge of the rift. A large guardian statue stands on either flank of the altar.

The rift extends an unknown distance both above and below the main cavern. The air in the rift is tainted by poisonous vapors (POT 80, resisted by Endurance; onset time is 1d6+3 rounds; failure causes Asphyxiation). The body of a nomad, large wounds visible upon his body, lies half in the rift. And two desiccated skeletons wearing tattered priestly robes lie close by.

The Fallen Priests

The two skeletons were once Lakadal and Werach, two priests of Tarsen who presided over the Mountain Foot Temple. Their shades are still present in the inner shrine and manifest to any living creature that enters. They originally died of starvation and are very hungry – they respond favorably to worshippers of Tarsen, and to offers of food (which in their case means the odor of food burnt as an offering). They can fill in details about the rituals needed to propitiate Khakun, and can provide Magic Points for the propitiation (they do not regain Magic Points

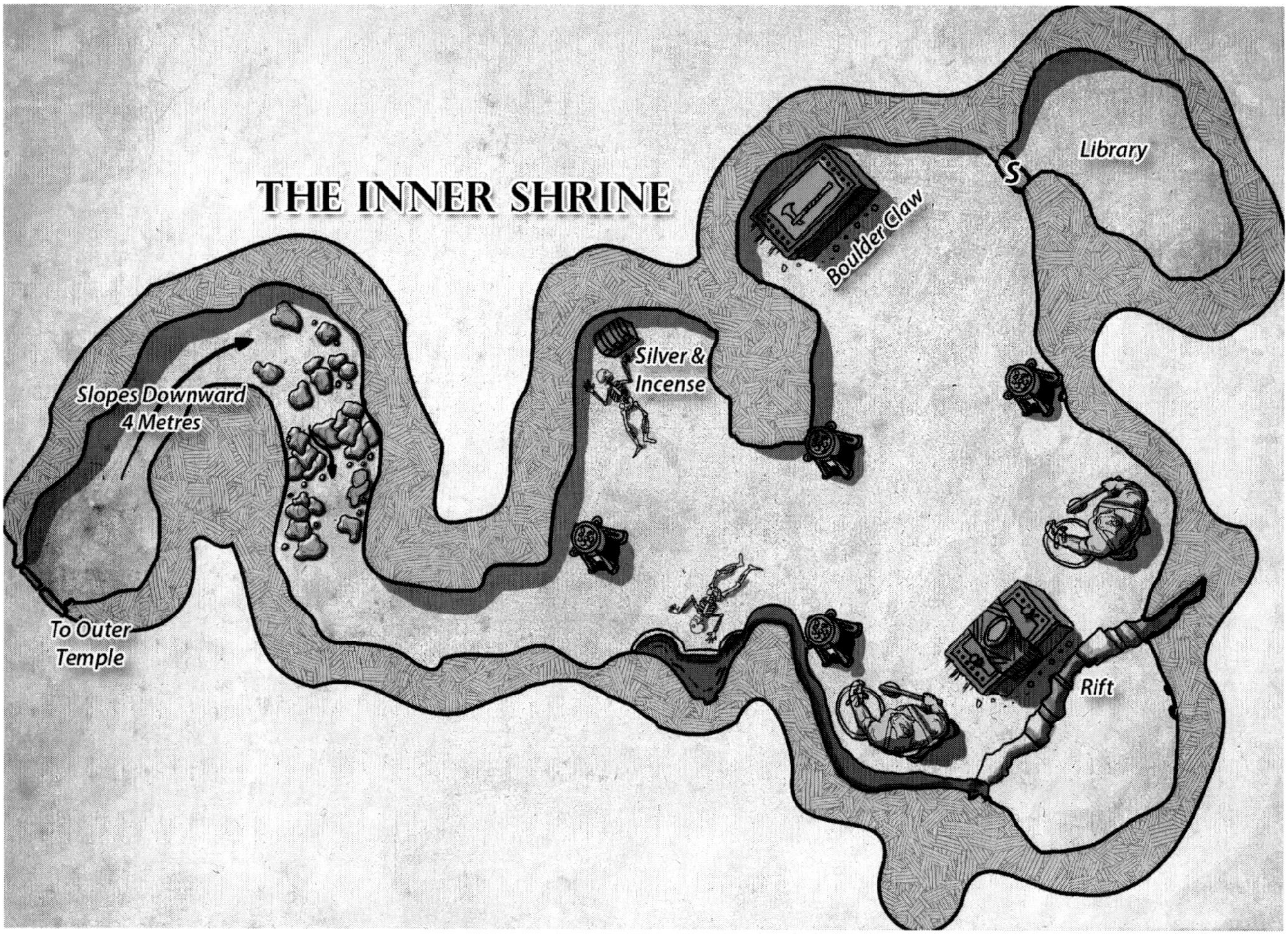

when Manifested, but regain them at a rate of one per week while they lurk in the spirit world). They can also explain that they killed the nomad when he entered, by driving him into the poisonous fumes.

Valuables

The inner shrine of the Mountain Foot Temple still contains several items of significant value:

- Boulder Claw: This is the sacred axe of the Mountain Foot Temple. It has a blade of excellent quality and an intricately carved haft decorated with gold and silver inlay. It inflicts +1 damage, has AP/HP 6/9, and is worth at least 500 taskeens.
- Silver Ritual Items: A locked chest contains a variety of silver ceremonial objects – circlets, chalices, jewelry and insignia – worth a total of 1000 taskeens. The original key is long-lost, so it can be opened either by picking the lock (opposed roll against the craftsman's 85% skill) or by breaking it open (the chest has AP 6, HP 12).
- Incense: The locked chest contains six jars of incense, each jar worth 50 taskeens.

Michel Tob, the two dead Tarsen priests, and any right-thinking Tarsen worshipper will not be in favor of looting any of these items. However, there are some items of value that they will not object to characters taking:

- The Lost Body: Some unfortunate explorer climbed down into the rift behind the altar, where he succumbed to the vapors. His body is still down there, clad in a bronze breastplate (AP 5, enc 8, covering chest and abdomen, worth 200 taskeens) and bearing a high-quality bronze broadsword (1d8 damage, siz M, Reach M, enc 2, AP/HP 8/12, worth 100 taskeens). Spotting his body requires a hard Perception roll. Retrieving his goods requires some ingenuity. The rift is 8 metres deep, and quite narrow – only someone of SIZ 11 or less can now squeeze into it. The body lies awkwardly at the bottom of the rift, and retrieving any of the items requires a Formidable Athletics roll for each item retrieved.

- ◐ The Dead Nomad: The Sheng nomad the two shades killed was carrying the standard armaments of a Sheng warrior (short spear, stone mace, compound bow, leather armor, and 20 arrows) plus a bronze and silver torc worth 30 taskeens.

Driving Out The Nightmares

When the characters have some level of control over the inner shrine, Tob prepares to perform the ritual to calm the giant; the characters are integral to the process. The ritual has eight roles, each of which depends upon a skill:

- ◐ ***Okonia***, Raven-tressed daughter of the giant Khakun (Taskan Rites)
- ◐ ***The Platter*** that bears delicacies to the giant (Customs)
- ◐ ***The Song*** that lulls the giant's sleep (Singing)
- ◐ ***The Nightmares*** that trouble the giant's rest (special, see below)
- ◐ ***The Incense*** that draws the nightmares from the giant's ear (Deceit)
- ◐ ***The Silken Shawl*** that tangles the nightmares' flight (Unarmed)
- ◐ ***The Bright Dagger*** that pierces the nightmares through (Combat Style, bladed weapon)
- ◐ ***The Fire*** that scorches the nightmares away (Willpower)

Someone must be assigned to each of these roles. One character may occupy more than one role, if necessary. Tob may also fill one role (Platter and Fire are most suited to his skills). There are two roles that have special requirements. The character who takes the role of Okonia must be a woman, or at least dressed like one and must have black hair. Finally, Tob has brought the convict Terceris Yando along for the purpose of playing the Nightmares. That role does not require the death of the participant, but it does require that he be captured, cut, and burned. Tob very naturally assumes that an involuntary participant would be preferable for such a role.

The Ritual

At each stage of the ritual, the designated character must make an appropriate skill roll and spend a Magic Point. If the character fails the initial roll, they may reattempt but the cost in Magic Points increases by one for each failed attempt (2 on the second attempt, 3 on the third, and so on). In all cases, one other person may use Taskan Rites skill to augment the character rolling. The augmenting character must also spend 1 Magic Point, but does not need to make a skill roll. The benefit is that the primary character's chance of success is increased by one-fifth of the augmenting character's Taskan Rites skill. If a character fumbles their roll, their reattempt and the roll of the next character are both one difficulty grade harder.

The steps of the ritual are:

1. Okonia calls upon her father, the giant Khakun. *(invoke the giant with a Taskan Rites roll)*
2. Bring delicacies upon a Platter to the giant to settle his stomach *(burn some food upon the altar with a Customs roll)*
3. Sing a pleasing Song to settle the giant to sleep *(sing an old song, a simple Singing roll)*
4. The Nightmares rage and disturb the giant's sleep *(the convict Terceris Yando is brought to the altar; he must scream and yell out)*
5. The Incense draws the Nightmares from the giant's ear *(burn incense upon the altar and persuade the convict to step away from the altar – Michel Tob intends to do this with a rope, but the character playing the role must make a Deceit roll)*
6. The Silken Shawl tangles the Nightmares *(bind the convict with a shawl with an Unarmed roll)*
7. The Bright Dagger cuts the Nightmares *(draw blood from the convict with a bladed weapon and a Combat Style roll)*
8. The Fire scorches the Nightmares *(burn the convict with a coal drawn from the altar, with a Willpower roll needed to hold the coal properly)*

Once the ritual is complete the giant Khakun is calmed and Tob (or any other Tarsen worshipper who knows the Propitiate spell) can negotiate with the giant's spirit to determine an annual price in Magic Points to keep the mountain stable. The annual ritual required is a simpler version of the ritual the characters carried out.

Emergence of The Nightmares

The ritual goes according to the guidelines above up to the point where the Nightmares rage. At that point, Yando is transformed and actual Nightmares emerge from the rift. At the same time, a force of Sheng nomads attacks the Taskan militia outside the temple.

As he transforms, Terceris Yando breaks any bonds the characters might have placed upon him. His features become monstrous and distorted. His body becomes shadowed and indistinct, growing and shrinking erratically with the play of the light and darkness within the cavern. One Nightmare for each character flies out of the rift, plus one for Tob and one for each of the Tarsen priests' shades. The Nightmares are of moderate size, with distorted heads and clawed hands. Their bodies trail away into wisps of darkness. They attack with claws and with their *Fear* and *Horrifying Dreams* powers, alternating from one to the other. The Nightmares are essentially twisted versions of Ethereals (Thennla source book, page 26), the ritual lending them physical form, so that they engage in physical combat.

The conflict outside between the Taskan militia and the nomads parallels that of the characters and the Nightmares – if the characters easily defeat their foes, the militia do similarly well. If the characters suffer losses or are defeated, the militia are overpowered by the Sheng.

Depending upon the roles they took within the ritual, the characters gain specific benefits when fighting the Nightmares. In particular:

- ***Okonia***: The character's defense rolls against Nightmares are one difficulty grade easier
- ***The Platter***: The character gains 3 additional magical Armour against Nightmare attacks. The Armour Points are applied to every Hit Location
- ***The Song:*** Nightmares must pay an additional Action Point to attack the character
- ***The Incense***: The character gains a free action to defend against Nightmares, and may pay 1 Magic Point to force a Nightmare to attack them
- ***The Silken Shawl***: The character automatically gains the Stun Location Special Effect against Nightmares
- ***The Bright Dagger:*** The character's cutting weapon gains a True (weapon) benefit when attacking Nightmares – roll damage twice, taking the best result
- ***The Fire:*** The character automatically gains the Bleed Special Effect against Nightmares

If the characters are able to defeat the Nightmares, the effect is the same as a successful finish to the planned ritual.

Conclusion & Rewards

If the characters are able to defeat the Nightmares, Khakun is settled and remains stable for a year. Tob (or the two shades, if Tob did not survive) are able to construct an appropriate Propitiation ritual for the following year. The base cost for the ritual is 50 Magic Points, plus 10 Magic Points for every character killed in the fight against the Nightmares. It should be noted that the Propitiation ritual is intended to be an ongoing settlement performed (and paid for) by others after the characters have left the area.

If the characters were defeated by the Nightmares, either all killed or driven out of the inner shrine, then no Propitiation of the mountain is possible for at least a year. If the silver mine remains open, there will be an earthquake strong enough to collapse it at some point over the coming year. If the characters suffered a complete defeat (all of them were killed), the earthquake is powerful enough to also devastate New Seppesh. The Kismek Sheng nomads who incited the mountain with their drumming rituals are on hand when the earthquake comes and able to capture and enslave hundreds of the colonists.

The characters may have picked up some items of value during the adventure. If he survives, Michel Tob insists that half of the value be turned over to the surviving Taskan militia and their officer. He does not complain if the characters think of this before he mentions it. If the characters refuse, then Tob is disappointed, and the enmity of the Taskan militia and its captain is guaranteed: life in New Seppesh could become very difficult for them.

Non-Player Characters

Michel Tob, Flamen of Tarsen, Zygas Targa Initiate

Michel Tob is a small man with more fat than muscle on his frame. He is very loyal to the Emperor and to his adopted city, but in a cheerful way that does not play well with the staid formality of his superiors. His formal robes are decidedly informal, and his gear has the flavour of age to it.

Tob	Attributes
STR: 8	Action Points: 3
CON: 13	Damage Modifier: -1d2
SIZ: 12	Magic Points: 15 (14)
DEX: 8	Movement: 6 metres
INT: 17	Initiative Bonus: 13 (10)
POW: 15	Armour: Ring & Leather
CHA: 14	Magic: Folk Magic, Theism

Skills: Athletics 36%, Brawn 30%, Devotion (Tarsen) 90%, Endurance 36%, Evade 36%, Evoke 90%, Craft (Brewing) 70%, Customs 90%, Influence 70%, Literacy 70%, Locale 70%, Tarsenian Rites 90%, Willpower 60%

Passions: Loyalty (Emperor) 70%, Love (Beer) 60%, Loyalty (New Seppesh) 60%

Magic

Folk Magic 90% (Bladesharp, Blessing, Bludgeon, Calculate, Disruption, Heal, Ignite, Lock, Repair, Sanctify, Worship (Tarsen), Worship (Zygas Taga)

Theist Magic – Tarsen (Devotional Pool 12) Consecrate, Inviolate, Propitiate, Tongues

1d20	Location	AP/HP
1–3	Right Leg	2 / 5
4–6	Left Leg	2 / 5
7–9	Abdomen	4 / 6
10–12	Chest	4 / 7
13–15	Right Arm	2 / 4
16–18	Left Arm	2 / 4
19–20	Head	4 / 5

Combat Style: Taskan Swordsman 60% (Broadsword,Target Shield; Formation Fighting)

Weapon	Size/Force	Reach	Damage	AP/HP
Dagger	*S*	*S*	*1d4+1-1d2*	*6/8*
Broadsword	*M*	*L*	*1d8-1d2*	*6/10*
Target	*L*	*S*	*1d3+1-1d2*	*4/9*

Captain Varhalle Eghis, Taskan Officer, Zygas Targa Initiate

Captain Eghis looms over his men like an ill-tempered bear. He has served the Empire for years, fighting against Sheng, Soribisi, Marangians, and many others. And for all that, he finds himself stuck in a backwater. He has unusually high loyalty to his men and does not want them to die under his command.

Eghis	Attributes
STR: 16	Action Points: 2
CON: 9	Damage Modifier: +1d4
SIZ: 16	Magic Points: 12 (11)
DEX: 8	Movement: 6 metres
INT: 13	Initiative Bonus: 11 (6)
POW: 12	Armour: Ring
CHA: 13	Magic: Folk Magic, Sorcery

Skills: Athletics 70%, Brawn 60%, Endurance 70%, Evade 60%, Invoke (Soldier's List) 50%, Lore (Strategy & Tactics) 60%, Oratory 60%, Shaping 40%, Tarsenian Rites 40%, Willpower 54%

Passions: Loyalty (Emperor) 50%, Loyal (Soldiers) 70%, Hate (Sheng) 80%

Magic

Sorcery (Intensity 5) Damage Boosting, Damage Resistance

1d20	Location	AP/HP
1–3	Right Leg	4 / 5
4–6	Left Leg	4 / 5
7–9	Abdomen	4 / 6
10–12	Chest	4 / 7
13–15	Right Arm	4 / 4
16–18	Left Arm	4 / 4
19–20	Head	4 / 5

Combat Style: Taskan Citizen Infantry 70% (Spear, Dirk, Militia Shield; Shield Wall)

Weapon	Size/Force	Reach	Damage	AP/HP
Spear	*M*	*L*	*1d8+1+1d4*	*4/5*
Dirk	*S*	*S*	*1d3+2+1d4*	*4/8*
Militia Shield	*L*	*S*	*1d4+1d4*	*6/10*

Habalbus Narassia, Taskan Sorcerer, Zygas Taga Initiate

Habalbus Narassia has a lazy sort of ambition. He recognized long ago that being a sorcerer attached to the Taskan army was a good way to get the cachet of the military without the risk (or most of the work) of actually being a soldier. And a posting like New Seppesh is even better – Imperial money is good, the colonists keep out of his way, and it is rare that he has to actually exert himself.

Narassia	Attributes
STR: 8	Action Points: 3
CON: 12	Damage Modifier: None
SIZ: 16	Magic Points: 14 (13)
DEX: 12	Movement: 6 metres
INT: 16	Initiative Bonus: 14 (11)
POW: 14	Armour: Ring & Leather
CHA: 12	Magic: Folk Magic, Sorcery

Skills: Athletics 32%, Brawn 24%, Customs 60%, Endurance 50%, Evade 24%, Invoke (Workings of Bountiful Earth) 60%, Shaping 60%, Tarsenian Rites 60%, Willpower 54%

Passions: Loyalty (Emperor) 70%, Loyalty (New Seppesh) 50%

Magic

Folk Magic 60%, (Bladesharp, Disruption, Heal, Protection)

Sorcery (Intensity 6) Abjure (Pain), Rejuvenate, Spell Resistance, Wrack (Nettles)

1D20	Location	AP/HP
1–3	Right Leg	2 / 6
4–6	Left Leg	2 / 6
7–9	Abdomen	3 / 7
10–12	Chest	3 / 8
13–15	Right Arm	2 / 5
16–18	Left Arm	2 / 5
19–20	Head	4 / 6

Combat Style: Taskan Citizen Infantry 50% (Spear, Dirk, Militia Shield; Shield Wall)

Weapon	Size/Force	Reach	Damage	AP/HP
Spear	*M*	*L*	*1d8+1*	*4/5*
Dirk	*S*	*S*	*1d3+2*	*4/8*
Militia Shield	*L*	*S*	*1d4*	*6/10*

Taskan Militia Member

These men are weathered and tough, but they are not professional soldiers. Their equipment is old and mismatched, a mix of salvage, military surplus, and whatever they could buy on their own. They are farmers, miners and labourers and very much look to Captain Eghis for guidance.

Militia	Attributes
STR: 11	Action Points: 2
CON: 10	Damage Modifier: None
SIZ: 12	Magic Points: 11
DEX: 10	Movement: 6 metres
INT: 12	Initiative Bonus: 11 (10)
POW: 11	Armour: Leather
CHA: 11	Magic: None

Skills: Athletics 50%, Brawn 50%, Endurance 40%, Evade 20%, Perception 50%, Willpower 22%

Passions: : Loyalty (Emperor) 60%, Loyalty (Militia) 50%

1D20	Location	AP/HP
1–3	Right Leg	0 / 5
4–6	Left Leg	0 / 5
7–9	Abdomen	2 / 6
10–12	Chest	2 / 7
13–15	Right Arm	0 / 4
16–18	Left Arm	0 / 4
19–20	Head	2 / 5

Combat Style: Taskan Citizen Infantry 50% (Spear, Dirk, Militia Shield; Shield Wall)

Weapon	Size/Force	Reach	Damage	AP/HP
Spear	*M*	*L*	*1d8+1*	*4/5*
Dirk	*S*	*S*	*1d3+2*	*4/8*
Militia Shield	*L*	*S*	*1d4*	*6/10*

Draubalhut, Sheng (Kismek) Leader

The Sheng leader is a whirlwind of a man, tall and scarred. His hair is long and braided. At night, his magic causes his eyes to glow with pale fire. He was too young to fight when his father and uncles overran Far Tarsenia and were driven back by Taskan blades. He will not see the same fate for himself or his tribesmen – he will wear the city-men down until they cry tears of blood.

***Nightmare-Infused Draubalhut**: For 1 MP, inspire Fear in a target as an attack Special Effect. The target may resist with Willpower against the original attack roll. For 2 MP, Darkness Step as an attack or parry Special Effect – the Sheng leader moves in such a way as to ensure the opponent cannot attack (but can defend) next round.*

Draubalhut	Attributes
STR: 13	Action Points: 3
CON: 16	Damage Modifier: +1d2
SIZ: 15	Magic Points: 13 (9)
DEX: 13	Movement: 6 metres
INT: 13	Initiative Bonus: 13 (10)
POW: 13	Armour: Linothorax, Half Plate
CHA: 12	Magic: Folk Magic, Fetishes

Skills: Athletics 66%, Brawn 58%, Endurance 52%, Evade 80%, Perception 85%, Riding 89%, Sheng Rites 70%, Survival 85%, Willpower 46%

Passions: Loyalty (Sheng) 80%, Hate Taskans 70%

Magic

Folk Magic 70%, (Bladesharp, Heal, Mobility, Twilight Sight)

Sheng Spirit Fetishes: Spell Ward 3, Luck Fetish

1D20	Location	AP/HP
1–3	Right Leg	2 / 7
4–6	Left Leg	2 / 7
7–9	Abdomen	4 / 8
10–12	Chest	4 / 9
13–15	Right Arm	2 / 6
16–18	Left Arm	2 / 6
19–20	Head	5 / 7

Combat Style: Kismek Archer 90% (Recurve Bow; Mounted Fighter), Kismek Lancer 70% (Long Spear, Short Spear, Buckler; Mounted Fighter)

Weapon	Size/Force	Reach	Damage	AP/HP
Long Spear	*L*	*VL*	*1d10+1+1d2*	*4/10*
Spear	*M*	*L*	*1d8+1+1d2*	*4/5*
Buckler	*M*	*S*	*1d3+1d2*	*6/9*
Bow	*H*	*S*	*1d8+1d2*	*4/8*

Sheng (Kismek) Nomad Rider

The Sheng riders are short and sinewy, with muscles honed by long hours in the saddle. Their armour and weapons are decorated with carvings, plumes of horsehair and long feathers. Those who have been drumming are streaked with sweat, with smeared decorations from the ceremony across their faces.

***Nightmare-Infused Nomad**: For 1 MP, inspire Fear in a target as an attack Special Effect. The target may resist with Willpower against the original attack roll.*

Sheng	Attributes
STR: 11	Action Points: 3
CON: 11	Damage Modifier: None
SIZ: 12	Magic Points: 10
DEX: 13	Movement: 6 metres
INT: 12	Initiative Bonus: 13 (11)
POW: 10	Armour: Leather
CHA: 10	Magic: Folk Magic

Skills: Athletics 35%, Brawn 35%, Endurance 32%, Evade 46%, Perception 50%, Riding 60%, Survival 40%, Willpower 30%

Passions: Loyalty (Sheng) 60%, Hate Taskans 60%

Magic

Folk Magic 40%, (Bladesharp, Mobility)

1D20	Location	AP/HP
1–3	Right Leg	2 / 5
4–6	Left Leg	2 / 5
7–9	Abdomen	2 / 6
10–12	Chest	2 / 7
13–15	Right Arm	2 / 4
16–18	Left Arm	2 / 4
19–20	Head	2 / 5

Combat Style: Kismek Archer 50% (Recurve Bow; Mounted Fighter), Kismek Lancer 40% (Long Spear, Short Spear, Buckler; Mounted Fighter)

Weapon	Size/Force	Reach	Damage	AP/HP
Long Spear	*L*	*VL*	*1d10+1*	*4/10*
Spear	*M*	*L*	*1d8+1*	*4/5*
Buckler	*M*	*S*	*1d3*	*6/9*
Bow	*H*	*S*	*1d8*	*4/8*

Sheng Horses

Tough mounts trained for battle, Sheng Horses are branded with tribal and clan fetishes, wear colourful saddlecloths, and have their tails plaited with leather thongs.

Sheng Horse	Attributes
STR: 22	Action Points: 2
CON: 13	Damage Modifier: +1d12
SIZ: 31	Magic Points: 7
DEX: 10	Movement: 12 metres
INS: 11	Initiative Bonus: 11
POW: 7	Armour: Hide
	Abilities: Intimidate, Trample

Skills: Athletics 50%, Brawn 85%, Endurance 65%, Evade 40%, Perception 45%, Willpower 35%

1D20	Location	AP/HP
1-3	Right Hind Leg	1 / 9
4-6	Left Hind Leg	1 / 9
7-9	Hindquarters	1 / 10
10-12	Forequarters	1 / 11
13-14	Right Fore Leg	1 / 8
15-16	Left Fore Leg	1 / 8
17-20	Head	1 / 9

Combat Style: Rear and Plunge (Hooves) 60%

Weapon	Size/Force	Reach	Damage	AP/HP
Hooves	*H*	*L*	*1d6+1d12*	*As for Leg*

Short-Faced Bear Mother

A massive, snub-nosed brown bear with a strong maternal instinct and desire to keep her cubs fed.

Maternal Berserk: *If her cubs are threatened, the bear mother will go berserk. Damage Modifier changes to 1d10+1d8, Action Points go to 5, natural weapon Siz becomes E, she is immune to the detrimental effects of Serious Wounds and Fatigue, and has automatic success in resisting any Special Effect applied against her.*

Bear Mother	Attributes
STR: 31	Action Points: 3
CON: 13	Damage Modifier: +1d8+1d6
SIZ: 44	Magic Points: 7
DEX: 13	Movement: 8 metres
INS: 13	Initiative Bonus: 13
POW: 7	Armour: Fur
	Abilities: Intimidate, Nightsight

Skills: Athletics 70%, Brawn 85%, Endurance 70%, Evade 45%, Perception 60%, Stealth 65%, Swim 70%, Track 65%, Willpower 45%,

1D20	Location	AP/HP
1-3	Right Leg	3 / 12
4-6	Left Leg	3 / 12
7-9	Abdomen	3 / 13
10-12	Chest	3 / 14
13-15	Right Arm	3 / 11
16-18	Left Arm	3 / 11
19-20	Head	3 / 12

Combat Style: Ursine Fury (Bite and Claw) 75%

Weapon	Size/Force	Reach	Damage	AP/HP
Bite	*L*	*S*	*1d8+1d8+1d6*	*As for Head*
Claw	*H*	*L*	*1d6+1d8+1d8*	*As for Arm*

The bear cubs are half the size of their mother. Modify their statistics as follows:

Action Points 2

Damage Modifier +1d6

Hit Points, as for the mother but 5 fewer Hit Points per location

Skills: Athletics 50%, Brawn 65%, Endurance 50%, Evade 35%, Perception 40%, Stealth 45%, Swim 50%, Track 45%, Willpower 35%

Combat Style: Ursine Fury 55% (Bite & Claw)

Lakadal and Werach, Shades of Dead Tarsen Priests

The marks of starvation scar the two ghostly priests. They are translucent shapes still clad in fine priestly robes, but bent and shrunken. Until they are fed their eyes are dark voids. Once fed, they assume the shapes they had in life – Lakadal is tall and imposing, Werach barrel-chested and bald.

Shades	Attributes
INT: 15	Action Points: 3
POW: 16	Damage Modifier: +1d2
CHA: 12	Magic Points: 12
	Movement: 6 metres
	Initiative Bonus: 13
	Armour: None
	Abilities: Manifest (1 MP), Psychic Attack (0 MP, 1d8 MP damage), Wraith Form (1 MP, 1d8 physical damage), Glamour (1 MP, 2 Senses, Magnitude 6)

Skills: Devotion (Tarsen) 90%, Manifestation 65%, Spectral Combat 75%, Unarmed 60%, Willpower 80%

Passions: Loyalty (Tarsen) 90%, Hunger 90%

Terceris Yando, Condemned Criminal

Terceris Yando is a big man, his frame ravaged by a life of debauchery, petty crime and harsh punishment. Nobody has explained his role in the expedition to him, and he expects the worst. He glares at all around him with resentful hatred and speaks only when forced to.

In his Nightmare Possessed form, Yando has the values indicated in parantheses, and the abilities noted below.

Formidable Natural Weapons (Claws), Regeneration (1 hp/round, every location), Aura of Dread (as below), Horrifying Dreams (as below), Immune to Bleed and Stun Location

Weapons: Icy Claws, ignore 2 AP

***Aura of Dread**: Upon first sight of him, onlookers must make an unopposed Willpower roll. On a failure, the character cannot act for one round. On a success, the character may act, but all rolls are one difficulty grade harder for one round. With a critical success, the character may act normally. With a fumble, the character may not act for 1d4+1 rounds.*

***Horrifying Dreams**: This effect costs 1 MP to invoke. Unless the targeted character succeeds in an opposed Willpower roll he will suffer 1 point of damage to the head per round until he makes an unopposed Willpower check or 6 rounds pass.*

***Immune to Bleed and Stun Location:** This ability does not work against the powers of the characters embodying the Silken Shawl and the Fire.*

Yando	Attributes
STR: 11 (15)	Action Points: 3 (4)
CON: 8 (12)	Damage Modifier: +1d2 (+1d4)
SIZ: 16	Magic Points: 12
DEX: 14 (18)	Movement: 6 metres
INT: 12	Initiative Bonus: 12 (15)
POW: 12	Armour: None (Transformed Flesh - 3)
CHA: 9	Magic: None

Skills: Athletics 60%, Endurance 40% (70%), Evade 40% (70%), Streetwise 70%, Stealth 60%, Unarmed 70%, Willpower 40% (60%)

Passions:: Love Money 75%, Hate Law 50%, Hate Work 80%

1d20	Location	AP/HP
1–3	Right Leg	0 / 5 (3 / 6)
4–6	Left Leg	0 / 5 (3 / 6)
7–9	Abdomen	0 / 6 (3 / 7)
10–12	Chest	0 / 7 (3 / 8)
13–15	Right Arm	0 / 4 (3 / 5)
16–18	Left Arm	0 / 4 (3 / 5)
19–20	Head	0 / 5 (3 / 6)

Combat Style: Basic Thuggery 50% (Dagger, Knife, Club; Improvised Weapons)

Weapon	Size/Force	Reach	Damage	AP/HP
Claw	*L*	*S*	*1d8+1d4*	*As for Arm*

Nightmare Spirits

The Nightmares are of moderate size, with distorted heads and clawed hands. Their bodies trail away into wisps of darkness. They attack with claws and with their Fear and Horrifying Dreams powers, alternating from one to the other. Although they are essentially spirits, the ritual has leant them physical form, and they engage in physical, not spirit, combat.

***Abilities**: Formidable Natural Weapons (Claws), Regeneration (1 hp/round, every location), Horrifying Dreams (as below), Immune to Bleed and Stun Location*

Horrifying Dreams: This effect costs 1 MP to invoke. Unless the targeted character succeeds in an opposed Willpower roll he will suffer 1 point of damage to the head per round until he makes an unopposed Willpower check or 6 rounds pass.

Immune to Bleed and Stun Location: This ability does not work against the powers of the characters embodying the Silken Shawl and the Fire.

Nightmares	Attributes
STR: 14	Action Points: 3
CON: 11	Damage Modifier: None
SIZ: 8	Magic Points: 14
DEX: 14	Movement: 6 metres
INT: 12	Initiative Bonus: 13
POW: 14	Armour: Tough Skin
CHA: 8	Abilities: Formidable Natural Weapons, Horrifying Dreams, Immune to Bleed and Stun Location
Skills: Endurance 50%, Evade 50%, Stealth 70%, Willpower 60%, Other skills 25%	

1D20	Location	AP/HP
1-5	Tail	3 / 7
6-10	Chest	3 / 8
11-13	Right Arm	3 / 5
14-16	Left Arm	3 / 5
17-20	Head	3 / 6

Combat Style: Nightmare Claws 50%

Weapon	Size/Force	Reach	Damage	AP/HP
Claw	*L*	*S*	*1d8*	*As for Arm*